BBC Children's Books
Published by the Penguin Group
Penguin Books Ltd, 80 Strand, London, WC2R 0RL, England
Penguin Group (USA) Inc., 375 Hudson Street, New York 10014, USA
Penguin Books (Australia) Ltd, 250 Camberwell Road, Camberwell, Victoria 3124, Australia (A division of Pearson Australia Group PTY Ltd)
Canada, India, New Zealand, South Africa
Published by BBC Children's Books, 2010
Text and design © Children's Character Books
74-79 by Trevor Baxendale
6-7, 26-29, 40-41, 58-63, 82-83, 48-49 by Justin Richards
10-11, 24-25, 32-37, 42-43, 66-67 by Oli Smith
Line art on 32-37, 58-63, 74-79 and 82-83 by John Ross
Colours on 32-37, 58-63, 74-79 and 82-83 by James Offredi
Illustrations on 26-29 by Tomislav Tomis
10 9 8 7 6 5 4 3 2 1

ISBN: 978-1405906944
Printed in Italy

CONTENTS

ADVENTURES IN SPACE AND TIME

Regeneration is a time of change and renewal. 2010 has brought a new Doctor to our television screens. Yet he's still the same Doctor as first appeared on television nearly fifty years ago. So much is new but so much stays the same.

The Doctor might look different. He might sound different. The way he does things varies. But beneath it all, he still has the same love of humanity, the same determination to see justice done and evil vanquished. New hair, new legs, new teeth and a new grin – but he's still the Doctor.

The TARDIS too has been renewed. Damaged by the traumatic regeneration of the Tenth Doctor as he changed into the Eleventh, it crash-landed on Earth and then repaired itself. Like the Doctor, it is different, but the same.

From the outside it has barely changed – a slightly different shade of blue, slightly different windows... But inside, the main control room has changed rather more. It still has a distinctive central console, and roundels on the walls. But otherwise it could be a different craft.

And the places that the TARDIS takes the Doctor are every bit as varied, exciting and dangerous as ever. It has journeyed to spaceships in the far future and Venice in the past; a modern-day Welsh village and World War II London... But, as the Doctor discovers, the TARDIS is on a journey to its own destruction...

As ever, the Doctor does not battle the monsters alone. In Amy Pond, he has found a friend and companion who has known him longer than most of his previous companions.

When the Doctor and Amy first meet, Amy is just a little girl. But her house has been attacked. She doesn't know it, but the alien Prisoner Zero has escaped through a crack in space and time and ended up in Amy's spare room – a room she can't even see or remember. With the TARDIS still repairing itself, the Doctor leaves Amy for longer than he intends – not returning until years later, when she's grown up.

Amy has been waiting years for the Doctor to come back. She's written stories about her 'Raggedy Doctor', drawn pictures, made dolls... Everyone else thinks he's just her imaginary friend – something she should have grown out of years ago.

But Amy knows the truth, and she never gives up hope that one day he will return. And one day, he does.

The Doctor is such an important part of Amy's life already that she accepts his offer of a trip in the TARDIS, even though she's getting married the next day! Together the new Doctor and Amy are the perfect team. He has a boyish enthusiasm that is held in check by Amy's sensible, down to earth character. His experience and wisdom are a counter to Amy's naïvety and wonder...

Together, they face villains and monsters every bit as dangerous and as terrifying as any the Doctor has faced in his previous incarnations. But just as the Doctor has moved on, so have his enemies.

None more so than the Daleks. As cunning and ruthless as ever, a group of Daleks has survived and tricks the Doctor into unleashing a whole new race of Daleks. These new Daleks, like the Doctor, look very different. But like the Doctor, they are just the same as ever. Just as deadly, just as scheming, just as ready to exterminate all other life forms.

Doctor Who has changed in many ways in the last year. But like the Doctor himself, at its hearts, it remains very much the same. If you're ready for danger, excitement, thrills and horrors, if you're ready for the trip of a lifetime, then stay with the Doctor – and read on!

Amy Pond

From their first meeting when she was just a little girl, Amy Pond waited years for the Doctor to come back and take her travelling in the TARDIS. It was definitely worth the wait! She's been back in time, visited a futuristic space station and met aliens that have been living on Earth all along. And there's still more adventures to come...

Top Five Amy Adventures

1. Creepy Crack
Until the Doctor turned up, Amy had no idea an alien prisoner had escaped through a crack in her bedroom wall and was living in her house!

2. Save the Whale
Amy proves she makes a great companion when she finds a way to save the last Star Whale on Starship UK.

3. Countdown
When Amy gets a Weeping Angel in her eye, she has to put all her trust in the Doctor to stay alive.

4. Choices
Amy realises how much her fiancé, Rory, really means to her when the Dream Lord forces her to make a difficult decision...

5. Forget-me-Not
Amy's memories of the Doctor bring him back into existence after the TARDIS explodes.

Did You Know?
Amy spent almost two thousand years trapped in a stasis lock in the Pandorica!

Rory Williams

Nurse Rory Williams is Amy's best friend from childhood and her fiancé. He's left behind when Amy goes travelling in the TARDIS, but doesn't realise as no time passes for him. When the Doctor pops out of a cake at Rory's stag do, Rory jumps at the chance to join them on their travels, unaware of the dangers that await him...

Top Five Rory Revelations

1. Hidden Horror

Rory is the first to realise that Prisoner Zero is impersonating hospital patients in order to blend in to the village of Leadworth.

2. Rory's Research

Rory shocks the Doctor by being the first visitor to realise that the inside of the TARDIS must exist in another dimension to the outside!

3. Dream Death

Rory dies for the first time in one of the Dream Lord's alternate realities, but fortunately it's just an illusion!

4. Reptile's Revenge

Poor Rory is shot and killed by Restac, the Silurian, when he pushes the Doctor out of the way to save him. But it's not the last we've seen of Amy's fiancé...

5. Plastic Fantastic

Rory turns up again in Roman times, at the opening of the Pandorica. But now he's an Auton!

Did You Know?

Amy used to make Rory dress up as her 'Raggedy Doctor' when they were kids!

DOCTOR WHO IN NUMBERS

Prisoner **Zero** is the first enemy the Eleventh Doctor encounters!

1 Time Lord – the Doctor is the last of his kind.

The Doctor has **2** hearts.

3rd time lucky – it takes the Doctor three attempts before he can finally take Amy with him in the TARDIS.

The death of the **Tenth Doctor** is heralded by **4** knocks.

The citizens of Starship UK are allowed to protest or forget about the secret of their ship every **5** years.

There are 5 new ranks of Dalek.

Amy is **7** years old when she first meets the Doctor.

Queen Elizabeth the **10**th (Liz Ten) is the ruler of Star Ship UK.

The Weeping Angels make Amy count down from 10 before they try to kill her.

This is the Doctor's **11**th incarnation.

The Doctor is able to regrow his body parts if he is less than **15** hours into a regeneration.

Isabella is only **17** when she is enrolled at the House of Calvierri.

The Silurians' subterranean city is more than **21** km beneath Earth's surface.

The TARDIS explodes on **26/06/2010**.

The Doctor visits Star Ship UK in the **29**th century.

Despite Amy's efforts, Van Gogh dies at the age of **37**.

River Song is imprisoned in cell **426**.

The Doctor is 906 years old when he regenerates into his eleventh incarnation.

Rosanna Calvierri tries to sink Venice in **1580**.

Winston Churchill uses his Ironsides during the London Blitz of **1941**.

The Doctor programmes the Silurians' hibernation chambers to reawaken them after **1000** years.

Rory follows the Pandorica for **1894** years.

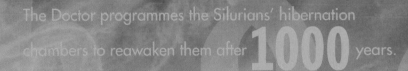

The Master uses the Immortality Gate

to create 6,720,949,338 versions of himself.

A CRACK IN TIME

From the moment the Doctor first meets Amelia Pond as a little girl, he can tell there is something special about her. The TARDIS crash-landing in her garden doesn't scare her, the madman that jumps out of the blue box doesn't scare her, but the crooked crack in her bedroom wall? That's a different matter entirely…

Amelia can hear a voice from inside the crack, a repetitive announcement saying that, "Prisoner Zero has escaped." It doesn't take the Doctor long to realise that there is a prison on the other side of the crack, and the reason Amelia is hearing the voice is because the prisoner has escaped into her house! However, with the TARDIS engines phasing, the Doctor has to save his ship before he can deal with the crack and accidentally comes back to help Amelia twelve years later. By this time, Prisoner Zero has been living in Amy's house undetected and has developed psychic links with a number of villagers to allow it to hide on Earth. When the Doctor helps the Atraxi prison guards finally catch up with their escapee, Amy thinks that is the end of the mysterious crack. But when the Doctor invites her to go travelling with him, she doesn't realise that the crack is also appearing on his TARDIS scanner.

There's definitely something strange going on.

It's not until they are trapped on the *Byzantium* by the Weeping Angels that the crack appears again. Examining the crack, the Doctor realises it is caused by an explosion so big that it is sending shockwaves backwards and forwards into every moment in history. The date of the explosion is the 26th June, 2010 and the light coming from the crack is the fire at the end of the universe. Time is literally running out through the crack. Anyone walking into the light is erased, never to have existed at all. The Angels think that, as the Doctor is a complicated space-time event, if he sacrifices himself then the crack will close. But the Doctor sends the Weeping Angels into the time field inside the crack instead, and it fades away…

Later, when the Doctor, Rory and Amy are leaving the underground Silurian city, the crack in the universe catches up with them again, appearing on the wall of the chamber they are in. Realising that where there is an explosion, there is shrapnel, the Doctor plunges his arm into the crack to see what he can find. He is terrified when he pulls out a piece of the TARDIS sign. Things look even worse for the Doctor and Amy, when a Silurian shoots Rory and the light envelops him. Rory disappears, never to have existed and to be forgotten by Amy.

But it's not the last they've seen of Rory and the origin of the crack is finally revealed when the Pandorica opens…

To find out more, turn to page 64.

Goodbye Leadworth, hello everything!

KNOW YOUR ENEMY

SMILERS AND WINDERS

In the 29th century, solar flares have roasted Earth and the entire human race has moved out to live amongst the stars. The residents of what was the UK are now living on Starship UK, under the reign of the queen, Liz Ten. The Smilers and Winders are the ship's security system...

Half Smiler, half human

Key hanging around neck to wind the ship's mechanisms

Ring shoots jets of smoke that can knock you unconscious

Security androids

Black monk-like robes

Demonic red eyes

Booths swing open to let the Smilers out

Face with three expressions – smiling, frowning, angry

SMILER

DALEKS

Long ago, Dalek Progenitors were scattered across space, containing a copy of the original Dalek genome. When the Doctor recognises some Daleks working for Churchill during the Second World War, his testimony is enough to activate one of the Progenitors, producing a whole new race of pure Daleks.

Taller than the old Dalek race

Colours denote five new Dalek ranks:

- Supreme
- Eternal
- Scientist
- Strategist
- Drone

WEEPING ANGEL

The Weeping Angels have the perfect defence mechanism - they are quantum-locked, which means they no longer exist in the sight of any living creature. But they are more than merely stone statues. Anything that holds the image of an Angel - a book or a film, for example - becomes itself an Angel. So whatever you do, in the presence of an Angel, don't blink!

Hands turn into sharp claws when they attack

Some of the stone Angels have eroded over time, but the radiation from the wreck of the *Byzantium* is restoring them

The Angels have no voices, but can communicate using the reanimated consciousnesses of people they have killed

Venom glands take twenty-four hours to recharge

Cold-blooded like reptiles

Forked tongues

Warrior classes wear body armour

Heat ray weapons

SILURIAN

An ancient Earth race also known as Homo Reptilia, the Silurians think humans are primitive apes. Their tribes live in suspended animation beneath the ground, following a prediction long ago from their astronomers that the moon would crash into Earth and cause an apocalypse. One day, they may awake and claim the planet as their own, unless both humankind and Silurians have evolved enough to coexist peacefully...

Their sharp fangs are still visible as their victim's subconscious can see that they are a threat and tries to alert the conscious brain

Like traditional vampires, they have no reflections

They use a perception filter to appear human

VAMPIRES

Although they look like vampires, the Calvierris are actually aliens from the planet Saturnyne. Their planet destroyed, they fled to Earth because of its oceans, as they need vast amounts of water to survive. Rosanna is the last female of her species, and is turning young human girls into Sisters of the Water, so that they can be brides for the ten thousand husbands that wait in the canals of Venice.

Clothes blend in to 1580s Venice

THE DREAM LORD

The Dream Lord is created by a mind parasite – a speck of pollen from the Candle Meadows of Karass don Slava – that falls into the time rotor of the TARDIS. The pollen heated up and induced a dream state in the team, feeding on the Doctor's darkest thoughts to create life-threatening situations for him and his companions.

Human appearance based on the Doctor's

No solid physical form

Definitely not to be trusted!

Finish ←

Start

GOING UNDERGROUND

The Silurians have a whole city beneath the earth.
Help the Doctor and Amy find their way through
this maze to the Silurians' laboratory.

All hail the new Daleks!

THE LEGEND REVEALED

Read the clues below and write the answers into the grid. The letters in the highlighted squares reveal the name of an ancient trap, built to capture the Doctor!

1. Who is the Eleventh Doctor's first companion? (3,4)
2. What is the yellow Dalek known as? (7)
3. The ship that River Song discovered a Weeping Angel on (9)
4. Isabella joined the Calvierri school. What was her father called? (5)
5. Who sets the Doctor, Amy and Rory a challenge to decide what is real? (5,4)
6. The name of the spacestation ruled over by Liz Ten (4,4,2)
7. What woke the Silurians from their hibernation? (5)
8. Prime Minister Winston's surname (9)
9. The alien that came to Earth to retrieve Prisoner Zero (6)

WHO'S THERE?

Use the clues to help you identify these shadowy aliens.

C. Keep your eyes on this one at all times!

B. These old enemies of the Doctor's are new, improved, and more terrifying than ever.

A. These creatures were hibernating deep underground until a drill woke them.

D. They look human but have a sinister mechanical side...

THE UNSTOPPABLE DALEKS

The Daleks are back, and this time they're more dangerous than ever before!

It is a tragic irony that the Doctor should have played a part in the rebirth of his most deadly foes, falling into a trap created by the last survivors of the Crucible – three Daleks who had escaped Davros and his reality bomb.

Desperately searching for a way to resurrect their race, the Daleks discovered the Progenitor, a device containing the means to rebuild the creatures in their most perfect form. But there was a problem. The Daleks who found it had become so impure during their genetic manipulations to stay alive, that they were no longer recognised. It was only thanks to a testimony from their nemesis, the Doctor, that the machine relented, and, in the bowels of the Dalek's damaged saucer, a new race was born.

Huge and imposing, these new monsters represent the Daleks at the height of their power.

Did you know...?

The Time Lords, wary that the Daleks might succeed in their plan to conquer the universe, wanted the Doctor to stop them from ever being created! But he failed, instead provoking a hatred of his race that escalated into the Last Great Time War.

Did you also know...?

Davros, the creator of the Daleks, eliminated all emotion from the mutated creatures except for the passionate hatred of anything that was different to them, to increase their chances of survival.

The Progenitor

Likened to a 'dandelion clock' by the Doctor, these devices were scattered throughout the universe during the earliest days of the Dalek Empire and contained the perfect genetic blueprint for the construction of a Dalek in its purest form. As a fail-safe, the progenitor can only be activated by another Dalek. By the time the refugees from the Crucible had recovered it, they had been so contaminated during their fight for survival that the machine could no longer recognise them.

Did you know...?
Apart from the Time Lords, the Daleks are the only other race in the universe to have mastered time travel.

Dalek Ranks

The Daleks' new, brightly coloured armour differentiates their different ranks.

White
Supreme.
No longer sporting the chunky gold and red casing that singled it out from its drones in the Crucible, this sleek white monster was born to lead.

Yellow
Eternal.
Like the Supreme Dalek, there is only ever one Eternal.

Blue
Strategist.
This rank control tactical planning and manoeuvring, coordinating the Drones during battle.

Red
Drone.
The foot soldiers of the Dalek army.

Orange
Scientist.
Their role is to examine and formulate new weapons as well as to analyse the genetic and physiological make-up of their enemies so that their weaknesses can be isolated.

You wanted to know what Gallifreyan fairytales were like, Pond, well, here you go! This is the one I told you about when we visited Vincent van Gogh!

Blind Fury

Sons of Gallifrey, Sleep No More!

In the Old Times, when even Rassilon was young, Death came to Gallifrey. He sent his messenger to a village in the foothills of the mountains of Outer Gallifrey.

The village was called Slothe, and the people lived up to its name. With every generation, the children became lazier than their parents. They had no thought for farming or trade, and no respect for the world around them. Why did they need to tend to crops, when the food they wanted grew in abundance in the forests and fields? Why should they bother themselves with farm animals when the wild broakir could be hunted through the foothills, and they could catch the singing yaddlefish in the rivers? The people picked the fruit from the silver-leafed ulanda trees and they raided the nests of the trunkikes for eggs and for young birds.

But for all their hunting and fishing, for all they took from the land, the people of Slothe never spared a thought to giving anything back. They enjoyed their easy lives, taking more than they needed. When the trees were bare, there were always more trees. When the river was empty, they found another. When the forest no longer echoed to the squeal of the broakir, they hunted further afield…

And over the years, the trunkikes moved to new nesting areas, and the yaddlefish swam in different rivers. The ulanda trees did not fruit and rotted away until only one was left… By their thoughtless actions, the people brought Death on themselves – brought Death's Messenger to the village of Slothe.

Three times, Death's Messenger visited Slothe. The first time, he came at night and bore away the souls of a dozen villagers. He left their bodies torn and broken. The people found their loved ones and their relatives the next day, and wept for their loss. For the first time, the people of Slothe were learning what it was to be without. They had gone without meat and without fish, without fruit and without fowl. Now they were losing themselves.

The second time Death's Messenger visited the people of Slothe, he came by day. But no one saw him, at least no one who lived. It was said that the people he slew saw Death's Messenger in the moment of their death. They caught glimpses of his teeth, his claws, his fury as he sought them out. They saw his shadow stretching out at sunset, and his reflection in the empty river, and they knew that Death had sent a monster to bend the villagers to his will. He passed through the village and left heartbreak and misery behind. His victims were the young, the strong, the healthy – and soon there was no one left to fight the monster.

No one, that is, except Presus, the son of the village prelate. Presus was the laziest of all the young men of Slothe. He slept until noon, and idled away the afternoons. He ate and drank the evenings away, staying up late with his friends and caring for no one but himself. Even the people of Slothe thought he was idle.

But Presus was the son of the prelate, and the strongest surviving son of Slothe. The villagers who had so far escaped the monster sent by Death came to see Presus. They came to beg him to find and kill the monster that Death had sent. But Presus sent them away.

They came again, and once more, the indolent Presus refused to listen to them. When they came a third time, Presus dismissed them and went down to the river to bathe.

He languished in the cool water for hours, giving no thought to the plight of his fellow villagers. Until, reflected in the water, he saw Death's Messenger. He saw the terrible claws and the hideous teeth. He knew that no one else had seen the grotesque creature and lived. Frightened for his life, Presus leaped from the water and ran. For all his laziness, Presus was strong and swift and silent, and he ran back to the village leaving the monster far behind.

He did not stop running until he reached his house. He closed and locked the door. Then he turned, and saw the figure standing in the shadows behind him. For an instant, Presus thought Death Himself had visited. But then he recognised the figure that stepped into the light. It was an old woman – the travelling Seer that Presus and his friends had mocked and laughed at.

The Seer was close to death. Her clothes were torn and her frail body was bleeding out its life from the wounds the monster had inflicted. Presus asked if she was hiding from Death's Messenger. But the Seer told Presus she was looking for him.

She told Presus that his life was coming to an end and that the village too was finished. But before he died he had a chance to do some good – to send the monster back to Death with a message from the village of Slothe and the people of Gallifrey. That message was that Death would not hold sway over them for ever, and that one day they would find a way to escape from Death's cold sleep. The sons of Gallifrey would sleep no more.

Her life ebbing away, the Seer took Presus out of his house, and showed him that the village was empty. While he bathed in the river, mindful only of himself, the monster had visited a third and final time. The Seer showed Presus where the last of the villagers had died at the claws of the monster. And Presus saw that the bodies were those of his own father and mother.

Then, at last, Presus understood his fate. In a blind fury, he took the long sword from the wall of the Opticon, the village meeting place. He covered his father's shield in leaves from the ulanda trees so that it shone bright silver in the light of the twin suns. When he was done, he turned to the Seer, hoping for her approval. But the old woman lay dead on the red grass outside the Opticon.

So Presus went in search of the monster alone. He followed it across the snowy slopes of the mountains, seeing its invisible footprints reflected in his shield. Finally, he tracked it to a cave at the foot of Mount Perdition.

The monster heard Presus approach. It came out of its cave, roaring and snarling. Reflected in the shield, Presus saw the monster turning this way and that as it tried to seek him out. It looked straight at him, but did nothing until Presus told the monster that he had come to send it back to its master, Death.

Then there was a mighty battle. Presus, armed with only his sword and shield, fought the monster with its claws and teeth. The young hero of Slothe watched the monster's reflection in his shield as he fought. He cut and thrust at shadows and empty air. Yet, in his shield, he saw the monster's yellow blood.

For three days and three nights they fought all across the foothills of the Mountains of Solace and Solitude. They neither slept nor rested, neither ate nor drank. Their breath came in ragged gasps, and their blood dripped from their wounds on to the white snow. But Presus fought with a blind fury brought on by the death of his parents and the fate of his whole village. He fought for them, not for himself.

For the first and last time in his short life, Presus the Indolent thought of others. He chased the monster across valleys and over hills, through forests and round lakes. He gave no quarter, felt no mercy, feared for nothing – not even his own life. Until finally, he thrust his sword deep into the monster's chest, and Death's Messenger was slain.

Then Presus threw away his shield. He broke his sword in two. Weak from the battle and from his wounds, he staggered back to the empty village of Slothe. With the last of his strength, he gathered his father and his mother and all the bodies and he built them into a great funeral pyre. It is said that when he lit it, the smoke from the fire could be seen across the whole Continent of Wild Endeavour.

As the flames died and the suns dipped below the snow-topped mountains, Presus at last rested. He lay down to sleep beside the funeral fire. And in that sleep, he dreamed of his dead father and mother and of the villagers. He dreamed of the Seer and of his fight with Death's messenger – of how he had defeated Death and fulfilled the Seer's prophecy so that the sons and daughters of Gallifrey need fear Death no more.

And Presus dreamed of the dark, shadowy figure that stood watching him through the dying flames – with an hourglass in one hand, and a broken sword in the other.

He is dreaming still.

GIANT
WORD SEARCH

All these words about the Eleventh Doctor's adventures appear in this massive word search. They might go forwards or backwards, horizontally, vertically or even diagonally. How many can you find?

Amy Pond
Atraxi
Byzantium
Crack
Cybermen
Doctor
Homo Reptilia
Leadworth
Liz Ten
Pandorica
River Song
Rory Williams
Sonic Screwdriver
Starship UK
Star Whale
Stonehenge
Supreme Dalek

TARDIS
Vampires
Venice
Vincent van Gogh
Weeping Angels
Winston Churchill

POLICE PUBLIC CALL BOX

POLICE TELEPHONE
FREE
FOR USE OF
PUBLIC
PULL TO OPEN

F	R	T	Y	U	H	G	S	C	R	A	C	K	Q	W	D	R	G	Y	A	K	I	J	G	S
W	N	B	V	C	X	D	F	G	H	Y	T	R	E	S	X	C	F	R	S	A	E	V	X	U
E	S	W	S	D	R	G	H	J	D	O	C	T	P	A	N	D	O	R	I	C	A	N	B	P
E	O	D	O	C	T	O	R	S	O	V	I	C	S	R	W	K	S	E	D	C	G	T	D	R
P	N	X	V	B	H	J	Y	T	E	F	D	A	E	F	U	Q	E	G	R	C	V	B	N	E
I	I	Q	W	F	S	G	T	C	H	J	E	K	L	P	U	J	N	O	A	D	A	L	E	M
N	C	W	C	H	E	J	U	Y	R	L	D	F	I	C	C	A	R	R	T	V	B	N	M	E
G	S	C	B	Q	R	N	E	I	A	A	W	H	W	S	D	Y	W	G	H	J	K	U	T	D
A	C	W	F	R	I	V	G	H	Q	E	S	B	H	U	W	I	B	L	N	T	E	F	G	A
N	R	V	F	T	P	H	W	B	V	R	A	X	F	I	G	T	Y	E	R	F	T	H	J	L
G	E	N	B	V	M	R	X	S	A	A	W	R	L	B	N	M	Z	O	R	O	Y	H	J	E
E	W	B	G	H	A	I	T	T	G	F	R	L	E	D	A	S	A	V	B	M	M	N	B	K
L	D	W	E	T	V	S	W	B	V	I	Z	A	X	V	F	N	R	F	Y	E	B	H	G	
S	R	V	S	B	G	E	M	J	K	A	O	A	D	P	O	K	T	A	M	E	Y	N	H	F
N	I	D	O	C	T	R	A	Y	M	P	O	M	W	N	D	R	I	V	S	I	N	G	L	I
B	V	H	B	V	F	S	P	S	N	E	I	Y	O	L	N	V	U	H	Y	T	G	F	D	A
G	E	V	M	J	U	O	C	X	S	A	U	P	R	L	Z	I	M	M	B	J	U	H	T	G
F	R	N	B	V	C	N	M	J	U	H	G	O	T	T	F	R	D	G	J	I	O	P	L	K
D	Z	C	G	T	H	G	N	O	Y	H	O	N	H	O	M	O	R	E	P	T	I	L	I	A
S	T	O	N	E	H	E	N	G	E	N	M	D	R	O	T	C	R	D	O	K	L	I	Z	T
K	N	Y	H	G	F	D	S	A	U	J	N	K	L	V	E	N	I	C	E	O	O	Z	N	B
V	I	N	C	E	N	T	V	A	N	G	O	G	H	H	L	L	G	R	H	M	A	T	A	I
H	B	G	Y	H	J	U	I	O	P	L	K	R	E	S	P	L	H	J	U	B	C	E	V	T
B	O	A	T	R	A	X	I	C	V	F	R	G	H	U	K	J	N	A	S	I	P	N	I	B
F	I	P	L	I	K	H	J	T	L	L	I	H	C	R	U	H	C	N	O	T	S	N	I	W

ZZZZZZZZZZZ

Daddy!

It won't budge!

Allow me...

A hornets' nest! They been there all summe I never got round to clearing it out!

What's in there? Quick!

Clunk!

Your own size...

All right hornets, why don't you try picking on someone...

Chipo!

ZZZZZZZZZ

Quick, get inside before they come round again!

Eek!

The question is, why didn't the chemical company realise what would happen?

Ahem.

Blimey, look at the bio-enhancing hormone level on these babies! No wonder you're in such a pickle!

Because it was developed in the tropics.

Where it's raining all the time.

That's it! The rain was diluting the chemical! Watering it down so that its effects were less extreme!

You are brilliant!

Well, duh!

Doctor! Where are you going?

Didn't I mention? I'm brilliant as well!

Amy, come with me. Rory, stand guard!

But what about the hornets?

Oh, don't worry about that Gero.

They're not the only ones with a sting in their tail!

What have you done?

Just a little atmospheric excitation! The rain should dilute the fertiliser.

Look! They're shrinking!

I think you'll find everything will be returning to normal now, nothing to worry about any more!

Thank you Doctor! You've saved our lives! But what about the rest of the fertiliser? What happens if the company keep sending more out?

Oh don't worry about that. I've a feeling they'll be getting a visit from the Health and Safety inspector very soon!

Goodbye Chipo! Don't forget to help your dad with the cleaning up!

Oh, he won't!

VWORP!

VWORP!

The End.

TIME TRAVELLER QUIZ

It's not just the Doctor that travels in the TARDIS. He is often joined by friends for journey through time and space. But which of the TARDIS travellers are you most like? Pick a starting point and answer the questions to find out.

START — Do you like to travel?
YES / NO

Are you always loyal?
YES / NO

Have you ever had an imaginary friend?
NO / YES

Are people sometimes scared of you?
NO / YES

If voting on Star Ship UK, what would you choose?
PROTEST / FORGET

Do you keep secrets?
NO / YES

START — Do you have a best friend?
NO / YES

Do people come to you with their problems?
YES / NO

Do you have anything sonic?
NO / YES

Would you give up everything for someone you have just met?
YES / NO

Do you wish you had more adventures?
YES / NO

START — Do you love where you live?
NO / YES

Do you have a caring personality?
NO

Do you like to tease people?
YES / NO

Are you ginger?
YES / NO

START — Are you mostly happy?
YES / NO

Has anyone ever called you mad?
YES

Do you ever pretend to be someone else?
YES / NO

Do you ever see things other people can't?

Have you ever met a Dalek?

YOU'RE MOST LIKE THE DOCTOR

With a keen sense of adventure, you're always ready to take on the next challenge, whatever it might be! Don't forget that travelling is always more fun with friends.

NO   YES

Do you sometimes crave a quiet life?

YES   NO

YOU'RE MOST LIKE AMY

Down to earth but always ready to discover something new, you're an excellent travelling companion. Sometimes your adventures might seem a little overwhelming, but try hard not to forget any important details, as they could save lives.

NO

Have you met your perfect partner?

YES

YOU'RE MOST LIKE RORY

Loyal and caring, you know that home is where the heart is and will do anything for your loved ones, even if it means putting yourself in danger. Make sure friends don't take advantage of your willingness to help.

Do you rely on technology?

NO   YES

YOU'RE MOST LIKE RIVER SONG

You're great fun to be around, but sometimes like to keep important information to yourself. Perhaps if you shared your problems with your friends, they might be able to help?

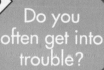

Do you often get into trouble?

YES

SCIENCE

YOU'RE MOST LIKE VINCENT

Your artistic temperament means that you can sometimes be difficult to be around, but your creative efforts are always amazing. You can be prone to sadness at times, but your friends can always cheer you up when you let them.

Do you prefer science or art?

ART

HOMO REPTILIA
– THE RACE BENEATH OUR FEET

Millions of years ago, an intelligent race of people evolved on planet Earth. But it was not the human race. We were just savage apes at the time, in the early stages of our evolution. We were seen as scavengers and pests by the true rulers of the planet, the cold-blooded Homo Reptilia – Reptile Men.

They have been known by many other names – Silurians, Eocenes and the less than flattering nickname Sea Devils. They built great cities and established an advanced civilisation. With their technology they could set up force fields, control other animals like dinosaurs and melt through rock...

They could also see into space. And their astronomers could tell that a small, rogue planet was heading towards Earth, on a collision course. The scientists predicted that the collision would be catastrophic. It would wipe out their civilisation. So they devised a plan to escape the coming apocalypse.

The Reptile Race built huge underground shelters, and put themselves into hibernation. They meant to sleep through the catastrophe and awaken once the crisis was over. But the reptilian scientists had got it wrong. The small rogue planet didn't crash into Earth at all. Instead it was captured by Earth's gravity and drawn into orbit. It became the moon.

So the reptile race slept on, through the millennia. Occasionally some of them have woken – by accident, or when disturbed by human activity, like the Discovery Drilling Project.

When the Doctor, Amy and Rory arrive in the small Welsh hamlet of Cwmtaff, the project has already drilled twenty-one kilometres into Earth's crust. It has already awakened a large colony of Homo Reptilia. Using their advanced science, the reptiles have drawn the bodies of the dead down from their graves, and captured Mo Northover.

The next stage of their plan is to cut off Cwmtaff with a force field, and assess the threat posed by this new, upstart race evolved from the ape pests. The reptiles are drilling back up towards the surface...

The Doctor has encountered Homo Reptilia before. Each time he has tried to broker a peace between the reptiles and the humans. But each time his attempts have failed, and ended in disaster. This time, he comes tantalisingly close to a deal. But again, the folly and stupidity, the lack of trust and the fear on both sides lead to a terrible choice. Once again, the Doctor is unable to secure peace. Once again, Homo Reptilia sleeps, waiting for the time when they can awaken and take control of 'their' planet from the upstart apes who have usurped them...

SILURIANS AND SEA DEVILS

The Doctor has met Homo Reptilia at least three times before. The Third Doctor first encountered a group that became known as Silurians when they were awakened by an underground scientific project. The Silurians released a plague to destroy mankind, but the Doctor was able to find a cure. He hoped to negotiate a peace treaty, but UNIT destroyed the Silurian base.

Soon afterwards, the Third Doctor discovered that the mysterious sinking of several ships was the work of a group of aquatic Homo Reptilia, who were nicknamed Sea Devils. Despite the Doctor's best efforts to make peace, the Doctor's old enemy the Master promised to help the Sea Devils reclaim Earth. The Royal Navy managed to destroy the Sea Devils' underwater base, but the Master escaped to cause more trouble for the Doctor...

The Fifth Doctor found himself caught up in an attack on the underwater Sea Base 4 by both Silurians and Sea Devils. They planned to launch the base's nuclear missiles and start a war in which the human race would wipe itself out and leave the planet for Homo Reptilia to re-inhabit. The Doctor managed to defeat them, but at enormous cost – the humans on Sea Base 4 perishing with the reptiles.

As always the Doctor was appalled by the loss of life, and knew in his hearts that there should have been another way.

THE IRONSIDE ADVANCE

With the new Ironsides now fully operational, the Battle of Britain lasted only one more week before the German Luftwaffe suffered crippling casualties and were forced to retreat, instead turning their forces against the Soviet Union.

But their underestimation of the strategic possibilities of the Ironsides would cost them dearly and, whilst their efforts were diverted elsewhere, the Ironsides landed on the Normandy beaches, travelling along the seabed of the English Channel to avoid detection. The conflict was brief, and soon the three Ironsides were marching across France, clearing a path for the liberation of the towns along their way by British soldiers.

Check this out, Amy! History as it might have been!

The enemy's guns were unable to penetrate the Ironsides' defences, and their speed and mobility meant that the Nazis were forced to retreat back to Germany to prepare a final defence. This allowed the Russians to spread across Eastern Europe at the other end of the allied pincer movement.

Up until this moment, the United States of America had remained strangely silent, unwilling to commit forces to a war that had seemed impossible to win, and instead steadily stockpiling their weapons until a tactically advantageous moment arose. But when the Japanese attempted to come to Germany's aid with a pre-emptive attack on Pearl Harbor, the Ironsides stepped in, taking on the enemy bombers in a vicious dogfight that lasted two days. The American Navy was saved and President Harry S Truman bestowed the Ironsides with a medal of honour, finally agreeing to aid the British in the war effort.

Two months later, the allied forces marched on Berlin, and the Nazi stranglehold was broken.

THE DEATH OF THE IRONSIDES

In the summer of 1942, the allies met in a secret war cabinet underneath Washington. With no common enemy to fight against, relations between the Soviets, Americans and British were breaking down and at the centre of the debate were the Ironsides.

Neither Stalin or Truman were keen to allow such powerful weapons to be the property of the British army alone, but the Ironsides' insistence that under no circumstances would they relocate from the United Kingdom meant that Churchill had no choice but to agree to their destruction.

It took the United States nearly a year to refine the nuclear technology needed to destroy Professor Bracewell's creations and, in an operation broadcast live across the globe, the first test of the atom-bomb took place on February 7th, 1943 on the Isle of Man. The Ironsides were vaporised in the blast.

WHAT HAPPENED TO PROFESSOR BRACEWELL?

Professor Edwin Bracewell (nicknamed the Scottish Boffin during the war years) was later knighted for his almost single-handed contribution to the allied victory in Europe. Sadly his genius was cut down in its prime, the destruction of the Ironsides devastating him to such an extent that he claimed he had forgotten key points from his research and work on such fanciful notions as "the gravity bubble" had to be abandoned. Relieved of duty once the war was over, he retired to a small town in the country where he is believed to have lived in seclusion for the rest of his life.

PROFESSOR BRACEWELL

CALL FOR THE DOCTOR

When Churchill tries t
phone the Doctor, to war
him about the message i
van Gogh's painting, th
call connects to one of hi
friends instead. Follo
the wiggly lines to wor
out who it reaches

THIS LAND IS OURS!

MASSIVE MONSTER MAZE

Guide Amy and Rory through the maze, avoiding the monsters as you go, to reach the safety of the TARDIS!

THE LONELY ASSASSINS

The following pages are all that remain of the definitive work on the so-called Weeping Angels, the Lonely Assassins.

It was written by Rastan Jovanich during his years of incarceration in the Insanatorium of Despard. Jovanich's notebook was found years later, hidden behind a loose brick in the cell from which he disappeared in the seventh year of the Ninth Concordance.

1

This I have discerned: That which holds the image of Angel, becomes itself an Angel.

Do not believe yourself to be safe if, like Perseus of ancient legend, you look only on the image or reflection and not on the Angel itself. A single image may not become fully Angelic. But a sequence or continuous motion of such images, unbroken by the blinks of the lens or the mechanism of a shuttered camera, can manifest as dangerously as the Angel itself.

Beware especially

2

...e touch of an Angel is said to chill the blood. It is like ice and stone and fear all compacted.

A single touch, a mere moment of contact, is sufficient for the Angel to steal from you the years that remain. They feed on your unlived life, your lost moments, the never-will-be and the won't-now-happen. Pray that your life will be over before you meet yourself, old meeting young. Reality and despair meeting hope and ambition. Because, if that happens...

3

Some may believe that if you can see an Angel then you are safe from its touch, from its curse.

But beware, for the eyes are not the windows of the soul, they are the doors. Beware what may enter there. Beware what may follow. Beware the Time of the Angels.

And, most of all, and this is of the utmost importance which it is folly to ignore, beware t...

4

Know only that you are not equal to the task. No one can stand against the Angels. We are all mortal, we all have lives unlived that may be claimed and taken by the Angels — by the Lonely Assassins.

No, there is only one who can stand against the Angels. Only one who it is said can meet the Lonely Assassins and walk away, unclaimed and unaffected.

Legend tells of the Lonely Traveller, the only man who could stand against and defeat the Lonely Assassins. His true identity is misted in myth and shrouded in uncertainty. But we know that he

5

This shall be my final page. I know that I must hide my notes, my precious book, before they come for me.

Above all else, that is my calling, my mission. Above even my own life. I have spent these last weeks prising loose a stone in the wall of my cursed prison — the cell in which I have been kept merely for speaking the truth. So much for my endeavours to warn the people of the danger they are in.

They see only statues, only Weeping Angels. But as I have set down here, they are not merely statues. And the Time of the Angels is approaching.

My cell door has been unlocked. The statue that was on a plinth in an alcove in the passageway outside is gone. I know not where, but I fear it is coming for me.

I must hide my book. Before the Angels

THE Sarah Jane ADVENTURES

Who is Sarah Jane Smith?

In her younger years, Sarah Jane Smith was one of the Doctor's longest-serving companions, accompanying him in his third and fourth incarnations. Sharp-witted and clever, she trained as an investigative journalist before meeting the Time Lord and her confidence and inquisitiveness often proved helpful during their adventures. She is the only companion to have faced the Daleks, Davros, Cybermen, Sontarans and the Ice Warriors!

After parting company with the Doctor, Sarah Jane returned to her old job as a journalist, until another encounter with the Tenth Doctor reinspired her to investigate and fight extraterrestrial attacks once amore – with a little help from her new young friends!

Alien Objects

Mr Smith

Mr Smith is a super-computer that Sarah Jane calls on when she needs facts and figures about alien species. He is a Xylok – a crystalline race that crashed to Earth thousands of years ago.

Sonic Lipstick

A gift from the Tenth Doctor, this device uses sonic vibrations to open any door that isn't deadlocked, just like the sonic screwdriver.

K-9

K-9 is a highly intelligent robotic dog, equipped with a laser weapon built into his nose! K-9 originally travelled with the Fourth Doctor, helping him defeat many alien enemies. The Tenth Doctor gave Sarah Jane her own model (Mark IV), with new, improved features.

Halkonite Puzzle Box

This super-strong, inescapable box is the perfect storage place for a Jeggorabax energy entity.

Warp Star

A gift from a Verron soothsayer, the Warp Star pendant contains enough energy to create a powerful explosion.

Scanner Watch

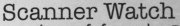

Another gift from the Doctor, this watch detects alien life and identifies origin and species.

THE Sarah Jane ADVENTURES

Sarah Jane's Friends

Sarah Jane is always grateful for a little help from her friends...

Luke Smith

Luke Smith

Luke is a very special boy. He was originally developed as an artificial human by the Bane as part of their plan to take over Earth. After he helped defeat the Bane, Sarah Jane adopted him as her son. Luke is supremely clever and has an amazing memory – although he is still learning about the world around him and can be very naïve!

Clyde Langer

Clyde is the joker of the team. Confident, streetwise and funny, he's also a little bit rebellious! Clyde started at Park Vale School at the same time as Maria and Luke and he lives with his mum. He likes football and art (although he keeps the art thing quiet, as he's worried it might not seem that cool).

Clyde Langer

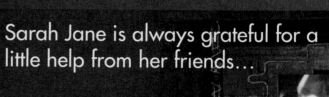

Rani Chandra

Rani joined Park Vale School, and Sarah Jane's gang, after Maria left for America. She is feisty, smart and headstrong. She wants to be a journalist, just like Sarah Jane, and looks up to her as a kind of mentor. Rani gets on well with both boys; she likes Luke for his intelligence and Clyde for his naughty charm.

Rani Chandra

The Doctor

The Doctor

Sarah Jane was reunited with the Doctor in his tenth incarnation, helping him foil the Krillitanes at Deffry Vale High School, and rescue Earth from the Medusa Cascade. The Doctor returned the favour at Sarah Jane's wedding, aiding her escape from the Trickster. During his regeneration, the Tenth Doctor rescued Luke from being hit by a car and waved silently to Sarah Jane as he entered the TARDIS. Although he didn't speak, Sarah Jane knew he'd come to say goodbye. But maybe she'll see him again soon…

THE Sarah Jane ADVENTURES

Sarah Jane's Alien Encounters

Sarah Jane's adventures introduce her to an array of extraterrestrial life forms – and not all of them are her enemies! Check out some of the good and bad aliens she's encountered...

Goodies

Name: Star Poet
Species: Arcateenian or 'Butterfly People'
Skill: Exceptional creative talent
Adventure: *Invasion of the Bane*

Benevolent and peace-loving, the ethereal Star Poet is a gaseous alien from the planet Arcateen V. She travels to different galaxies with her beautiful poetry. Sarah Jane met the Star Poet when she lost her way on Earth. In exchange for helping her return home, the Star Poet gave Sarah Jane a special superluminal communicator, which helped her defeat the Bane Mother.

Name: Eve
Race: Unknown
Skill: Can read and manipulate timelines
Adventure: *The Mad Woman in the Attic*

Rani found telepathic humanoid Eve hiding in a scary disused funfair in Danemouth. She'd taken control of some local kids – but only because she was lonely! The young alien had been evacuated during the Time War, when most of her race were killed by the Daleks. Sarah Jane and the gang helped Eve find her ship and return home.

Name: Captain Tybo
Species: Judoon
Skill: Highly motivated and well-trained
Adventure: *The Prisoner of the Judoon*

The Judoon are a kind of intergalactic alien police force! Heavily armoured, they look like rhinos and enforce the law of the Shadow Proclamation. Captain Tybo came to Earth in pursuit of escaped prisoner Androvax and the kids helped him recapture the evil Veil. The Doctor has also met the Judoon on a number of occasions.

THE Sarah Jane ADVENTURES

Sarah Jane's Alien Encounters

Baddies

Name: The Pied Piper
Species: Energy Entity
Skill: Shape-shifting
Adventure: *The Day of the Clown*

This evil energy entity from the Jeggorabax Cluster manifests itself in different guises, feeds off the emotion of fear and kidnaps children. When it first crash-landed on Earth, it took the form of the Pied Piper and later appeared as Elijah Spellman and Odd Bob the Clown. Sarah Jane weakened the entity by laughing at it and trapped it inside a meteorite, which she keeps in a container in her attic!

Name: Androvax the Annihilator
Species: Veil
Skill: Can inhabit human host bodies
Adventure: *The Prisoner of the Judoon*

The last remaining example of the ancient Veil species, the fugitive Androvax escaped when a Judoon prison ship crashed on Earth. Wanted in five galaxies for destroying twelve planets, Androvax is highly destructive and remorseless. He possessed Sarah Jane's body and tried to build a spaceship to escape the Judoon and destroy Earth, but was rearrested just in time.

Name: The Trickster
Species: Unknown
Skill: Can influence history
Adventures: *Whatever Happened to Sarah Jane?; The Temptation of Sarah Jane Smith; The Wedding of Sarah Jane Smith*

A member of the Pantheon of Discord, the Trickster is an extra-dimensional being who exists outside of time and space. He strikes bargains with humans who are about to die, altering the course of history and causing chaos. The Trickster caused Sarah Jane trouble twice before, then returned to bring more mayhem – this time at her wedding! With a little help from the Doctor, Sarah Jane was saved when her fiancé sacrificed his life for her.

SECRET OF ARKATRON

'Now, there's something you don't see every day,' the Doctor said.

The TARDIS had landed on a barren asteroid, a huge lump of craggy rock floating in space. The first surprise was that the asteroid had a breathable atmosphere. Standing a short distance from the TARDIS, Amy and the Doctor were looking at the second surprise.

The dark, rocky landscape stretched out to the horizon. Stars and other asteroids hung in the black sky. On a plateau across a shallow valley, silhouetted against the pale light from a nearby sun, stood a house.

'Spooky,' Amy said.

The house was old. It was built from dark, crumbling stone. Gargoyles perched under the eves, weathered by years of keeping watch. The steps up to the front door were chipped and discoloured like the teeth of an ancient skull. Blank, shuttered windows stared blankly back at Amy and the Doctor.

'Scooby Doo wouldn't be seen dead in there,' Amy said.

'Scooby Doo's a pussycat,' the Doctor told her.

'Well, OK, I know he's a dog, but he's a scaredy-cat-dog. Come on, let's go and explore.' His eyes lit up with excitement. 'Who knows, maybe we'll meet a ghost or two.'

It was further than it looked to the house. By the time they had climbed up to the plateau, Amy was out of breath. The Doctor, as enthusiastic as ever, led the way up the steps.

There was no knocker or doorbell. Something was carved in the cracked and flaking stonework above the door. It looked like 'Arkatron', but Amy couldn't be sure.

'You think anyone lives here?' Amy wondered.

'Why build a house if you're not going to live in it?'

'They might have moved,' Amy said. 'I would.'

The door creaked ominously when the Doctor opened it, just as Amy had guessed it would. Inside was a wide entrance hallway. It was lit with wall lights. They flickered and sputtered like candles and cast an uneven light across everything.

A flight of wooden stairs rose to a darkened upper floor. The steps were rotted and several

had fallen away. The uneven floorboards under
Amy's feet creaked as she walked. There were
several rooms off the hallway, and a wide
corridor leading past the stairs deeper into the
house. Several dusty suits of armour stood silent
and still in alcoves.

'Look at this,' the Doctor called. 'This is clever.'
He was standing in front of what looked like
an empty picture frame. As Amy joined him, an
image shimmered into view within the frame. A
video played, black and white, jumpy, obviously
very old.

'It detects movement,' the Doctor explained.
The video showed what looked like a political
speech. A man in military uniform stood on
a podium. There was no sound, but he was
obviously speaking with passion – waving his
fist, snarling with rage and anger. Behind
the speaker, other people nodded seriously in
agreement. A short man with round-framed
glasses and no hair peered out from between
two uniformed soldiers. A woman in a formal
dress clapped her hands.

'Clever,' Amy agreed. 'But boring.'
There were several more of the video picture
frames, as well as some normal photos and
paintings. They were all just as boring, Amy
decided.

The Doctor had already lost interest in the
pictures. He was tracing a wire round a
doorframe and across the wall. 'Alarm system,'
he told Amy. He found a small metal box close
to the front door. It was hanging broken from its
fixings.

'It's as old as everything else,' Amy said.
The Doctor shook his head. 'This is recent
damage. Someone disabled it, though I could
easily hook it up again.' He brandished his sonic
screwdriver. 'And look...' the Doctor pointed at
the floor. 'Footprints in the dust – and not just
ours.'

From somewhere deeper in the house Amy
heard a heavy creaking sound. Like a footstep.
'There is someone else here,' she said. She
closed her eyes, hoping to hear better as the

creaking continued. 'Definitely footsteps.' She
opened her eyes.

And found that the Doctor was gone. Typical.
Amy hurried along the corridor, towards where
the noise had come from. It ended in a large,
wooden door. Amy reached out, and at the touch
of her hand, the door immediately swung open.

'Doctor – are you in there?'
Amy stepped into the room. A pale, misshapen
figure rose up in front of her. It took a rasping,
throaty breath and reached out towards Amy.

Amy gasped and took a step backwards. Hands grabbed her from behind. She twisted quickly away.

'Easy, easy,' the Doctor said. 'It's only me. You look like you've seen a ghost.'

Amy was about to tell him that she had. But the white figure was reaching up to its misshapen head. It pulled off what Amy could now see was a protective headpiece, like a helmet made of flexible plastic with a breathing filter. Beneath the helmet was an elderly man with white hair and a moustache.

The man sighed and shook his head. 'I don't know why we bothered suiting up,' he said angrily. 'Miss Crisp!' he called. 'Come and look at these two amateurs who have bumbled in.'

'Bumbled in?' the Doctor echoed. 'Amateurs?'

The man stared back at him. 'You've contaminated the whole site, you know that? Amateurs.'

A figure wearing an identical protective suit appeared out of the shadows at the edge of the room. It too removed the helmet. Miss Crisp was not much older than Amy, and shook her head to free her long dark hair.

'That's better,' she said, taking a deep breath. 'It gets so hot in there. Don't let Professor Landale intimidate you. He's rather precious about his site.'

'I won't,' the Doctor said. He walked into the room and looked round. 'Oh, I like this.'

Amy followed and now she could see that they were in an enormous library. The walls were lined with bookshelves. In alcoves between the books stood suits of dusty armour like she'd seen in the hallway. There were pictures and video frames too, scattered in amongst the bookcases.

Like the pictures and videos in the hall, they all showed speeches, or generals overlooking a battle, or some sort of ceremonial occasion. Amy recognised the same general in several of them. The woman in the dress appeared in another video clip. A short, bald man was visible from behind, watching a town bombed by strange-looking aircraft...

'We found this place,' Landale said. 'We have first salvage rights.'

'No problem,' the Doctor replied. 'We're just visiting.'

'If you're not scavengers, then what are you doing here?' Landale demanded.

'Scavengers?' Amy asked, from across the room.

'People who would strip this place bare and sell the contents,' Miss Crisp said. 'With no respect for the historical value.'

'We think it must have been a museum or a gallery. Of course we've only just got here,' Landale went on, 'but everything will be properly catalogued.'

'It's all from the same period,' the Doctor said,

ooking round. 'The pictures, videocasts, books…'

'It's perfect, isn't it?' Landale said. He joined he Doctor and together they examined a shelf of books. 'They all seem to be records of court proceedings. I'm seriously thinking about renovating the house and opening it to the public.'

'Better than stripping everything out and selling t,' the Doctor agreed. 'I assume you disabled the alarms, by the way?'

'That was me,' Miss Crisp admitted. 'It's a complex system. It was routed right through the house, not just to sensors but receivers as well. So, better safe than sorry.'

'Didn't want to run up against some ancient defence system,' Landale added.

Amy had found a large framed photograph of a line of armoured vehicles driving past what looked like a palace.

Soldiers marched alongside. On a balcony, overlooking the parade, was one of the generals Amy had seen before. Beside him stood several other military figures, both men and women. The exception was a bald man in a business suit and wearing glasses. His slight figure was almost lost in amongst the more imposing dignitaries.

Next to the picture was an alcove. One of the suits of armour stood in the shadows. The blank metal visor over the face, like the rest of the armour, was peppered with dark spots of rust. The whole thing was dulled by dust. Without really thinking about it, Amy reached out and brushed away a cobweb from the breastplate. The metal was cold and slightly rough under her fingers.

Dust showered down. Amy realised it had fallen from the helmet, as the figure turned slowly towards her. The suit of armour took a clanking step forwards. Metal gauntlets clenched and unclenched, reaching out towards Amy. She backed away in horror from the faceless metal figure lurching towards her.

The metal hands of the walking armour grabbed Amy's shoulders, dragging her towards the faceless creature.

Then, suddenly, the grip on her shoulders relaxed and Amy tore herself away. Across the room, the Doctor was aiming his sonic screwdriver at the armour. It seemed to stagger, and then the legs gave way. The heavy metal creature crashed to the ground, sending up a cloud of dust.

'What was it?' Amy gasped. 'Was it alive?'

'I don't think so, not really,' the Doctor said. He bent down to examine the metal figure.

'A robot?' Professor Landale suggested.

'Must be,' Miss Crisp agreed. 'It activated when Amy touched it.'

'Local detection,' the Doctor agreed. 'But it was probably connected to the alarm system. Good job you turned it off.'

'Good job you didn't reconnect it,' Amy told the Doctor.

'Still could,' the Doctor boasted. He tossed his sonic screwdriver in the air, and caught it in his jacket pocket.

'Show off!' Amy told him.

Miss Crisp was examining the alcove. 'This isn't like the others,' she said. 'There's a door at the back – look.'

'Do you think that thing was guarding whatever's behind this door?' Professor Landale asked.

'Easy way to find out,' the Doctor said. Amy followed the Doctor into the room beyond. was a large bedroom, hanging with cobwebs nd covered in dust. In the middle of the room ood a large four-poster bed, the curtains round hanging in tatters. There was a slight hollow in he mattress, as if someone had just got up.

A video-frame opposite the bed showed a list f names. The list was headed 'Lest You Forget', nd the names below scrolled endlessly past ke a roll call.

On the wall opposite the door was an ancient painting, darkened with age. It showed a man being taken in chains through the hallway of a house. Stairs swept up to a second floor, and a corridor led into the depths of the house. The prisoner was seen only from the back, his bald head gleaming in the lamplight as he was led away by soldiers in armour rather like the suit that had attacked Amy.

Several more of the creepy suits of armour stood against the walls. Amy watched them closely, but none of them showed any signs of life.

Then she saw movement at the back of the room. But it wasn't another suit of armour. An unremarkable-looking man stood up and moved into the light. He was short, dressed in a crumpled suit, and wearing small round spectacles. He ran his hand over his bald scalp, as if smoothing down hair he no longer had, and looked round at Amy and the others.

'What are you doing here?' he asked, his voice unexpectedly strong and deep.

'Just visiting,' the Doctor said. 'Who are you?'

'I am the curator of this museum. My name is…' The man hesitated, glancing over towards the video-frame on the other side of the room before going on: 'Lester Forge. Forgive me, it's so long since we had any visitors here at the Museum of the Ninth Dynasty of Arkatron. But you are welcome to look round.'

'The Ninth Dynasty of Arkatron?' Landale said. 'Now that was an interesting, if rather bloodthirsty, regime.'

'The time of the dictators,' the Doctor said quietly.

'Well, I'm happy to look round,' Amy said.

There was another door just a few steps away and she went over and opened it. The curator called out to her. But whatever he said was lost in Miss Crisp's scream, as the body of an elderly grey-haired woman toppled through the doorway and landed at Amy's feet.

The Doctor was there at once. 'Let me see. She was slumped against the door, and fell through when you opened it.'

'Is she dead?' Amy asked.

The Doctor nodded grimly. 'Shot at close range with an impulse blaster. Poor lady.' He looked up at the curator. 'Do you know who she is?'

The curator nodded. 'It's Miss Dellman, my assistant. Whatever can have happened?'

The Doctor stood up slowly and turned to face everyone. 'I think it's obvious what's happened. Someone in this house is a murderer. And,' he went on, 'I know who it is.'

'Who?' Amy asked.

'Oh come on, Pond,' the Doctor said. 'Look around you. There are clues everywhere. You should be able to work out what's really happened here, and who the culprit is.'

HAVE YOU GUESSED THE SECRET OF ARKATRON?
TURN TO PAGE 82 TO FIND OUT.

LEGEND OF THE PANDORICA

The legends of the Pandorica date back to the very beginning of time. It has been lost for millennia, forgotten for aeons...

But when the Doctor realises the truth about the mysterious crack in time he keeps encountering, it is time for the Pandorica to open.

Buried beneath Stonehenge, the Pandorica is an ancient container. It is said to house the body of a great warrior. But, in fact, it is a trap – a trap for the Doctor. He may not see himself as a warrior, but that is how his enemies regard him. The Doctor is about to discover that nothing is what it seems or what he thinks.

It isn't just the Doctor who knows about the Pandorica. Numerous alien races gather to witness the event. The Doctor's greatest enemies come to Stonehenge in Roman times to see what will happen, or so the Doctor thinks. The Daleks, the Cybermen, the Judoon, the Nestenes with their plastic Autons and many, many more.

But the real reason they are here is very different. They have set a trap – a trap for the Doctor. A trap they hope will save all of creation... The Doctor's friends try to warn him of the danger he is in – Vincent van Gogh paints it in a picture, and Winston Churchill tries desperately to contact the Doctor. Because they know that the TARDIS itself is in danger. Its destruction will create the terrible fracture in time that the Doctor has been investigating.

And Amy is at the heart of it all. The Doctor first encountered the crack on her bedroom wall. The trap set for the Doctor is built from her memories... Even Amy's fiancé Rory is recreated from Amy's mind – an Auton, recreated as a Roman soldier.

But he becomes far more than that. When Amy is killed, and the Doctor puts her body inside the Pandorica to recover, the Auton Rory waits with the Pandorica for centuries. Called 'The Lone Centurion' by those who see him through the ages, Rory guards and protects the Pandorica – but really he is guarding and protecting Amy inside it. He is waiting until the Pandorica opens and Amy is restored.

The power of the Pandorica is awesome. It is enough to bring back to life a Dalek that has been turned to stone, as history itself collapses and the universe nears its end. Still seeing the Doctor as its greatest enemy, and desperate to exterminate him, the stone Dalek pursues the Doctor and his friends through a modern museum. Until the Doctor's old friend River Song destroys it.

But despite everything the Doctor can do, the universe is still in danger. With the help of Amy, Rory and River Song, the Doctor is desperate to stop his TARDIS from exploding.

When he finds he can't stop the inevitable explosion, the Doctor comes up with another plan. But it is a plan that means the TARDIS will be destroyed and the Doctor himself will never have existed at all…

Only River Song seems to remember him. On their wedding day, River Song leaves Amy and Rory a clue – a memento of the Doctor. The Doctor himself has also planted clues of his own existence in Amy's memory – going back to their adventure with the Weeping Angels to urge her to remember him… If only Amy can remember him, then the Doctor will be restored – just as Rory was recreated from Amy's memories.

Sure enough, Amy remembers. Right in the middle of her wedding reception, she remembers her imaginary friend – the Raggedy Doctor, with whom she and Rory have had so many adventures.

And suddenly he isn't imaginary any longer. The TARDIS materialises at the wedding reception – and the Doctor is back!

But the danger isn't over. Whatever caused the TARDIS to explode is still out there. Somewhere. But with the help of Amy and Rory, the Doctor is determined to find it…

HISTORY'S HEROES

The Doctor makes a habit of meeting his heroes, and often happens to bump into the stars of yesteryear on his travels through Earth's history...

The Doctor often meets royalty on his travels – Queen Elizabeth I once demanded that the Tenth Doctor's head be cut off and there's a chance he may even be married to her! And we've yet to see whichever mysterious royal called the TARDIS telephone on Amy and Rory's wedding day!

Winston Churchill

The most iconic of British Prime Ministers, Winston Churchill seems to share a special friendship with the Doctor, including possession of the TARDIS's telephone number! During the height of the London Blitz, Winston found himself unwittingly embroiled in a sinister plan by the Daleks. His war cabinet was transformed into a trap for the Time Lord, as the Doctor was tricked into revealing the creatures for the evil aliens they really were and so triggered their resurrection!

Vincent van Gogh

One of the most popular artists who ever lived, Vincent was unappreciated in his own time. His strange use of colour and texture as well as his eccentric behaviour made him the target of mockery in his hometown, but his curse was far worse than that, as he found himself able to see the invisible alien Krafayis that stalked the citizens near the Café Terrasse, his favourite haunt. With the Doctor and Amy's help, he defeated the creature and was brought to the present day to observe the impact he would make on the world after he died, but despite his best efforts, Amy never did accept his hand in marriage!

Agatha Christie

Unlike van Gogh, Agatha Christie was a star for most of her life and the toast of many a 1920s garden party. When she found herself embroiled in a series of murders that seemed to scarily resemble the plot of one of her novels, Agatha was forced to put all her wits to the test and, with the help of the Doctor and Donna, she managed to solve the mystery of both the infamous Unicorn and an alien Vespiform. It was only after the giant wasp had been defeated that the Doctor realised he had solved another puzzle; the reason for Agatha's strange eleven-day disappearance in 1926...

William Shakespeare

When the Doctor took Martha to the Globe Theatre in 1599, she was shocked to discover that, far from the proper and stuffy image that the history books had conveyed, Shakespeare was a roguish and rather good-looking man of the people! Clever enough to see through the psychic paper, he became the puppet of an evil group of aliens known as the Carrionites, who had developed a science based on words. They forced him to rewrite the end of his lost play, *Love's Labour's Won*, so that their race could escape into our universe, but at the last minute, Martha and the Doctor trapped them in their own crystal ball with a line from a *Harry Potter* book!

Charles Dickens

The Ninth Doctor bumped into Charles Dickens on Christmas Eve 1869, just in time to rescue him from the gaseous Gelth who had interrupted his reading of *A Christmas Carol*. Fascinated by the supernatural, Charles was able to return the favour when the Doctor and Rose found themselves trapped in the basement of a funeral parlour, forcing the creatures to abandon the animated corpses they had possessed by filling the house with gas! Charles was so inspired by the events of that night that he vowed to write them down in his next book, but sadly he died before its completion.

Queen Victoria

During her pilgrimage to Scotland, Queen Victoria was trapped in the Torchwood Estate by a group of warrior monks and their werewolf. Together with the Doctor and Rose, the Queen discovered that her late husband had investigated the local legends and created a trap within a trap to protect her. Using a huge telescope, the Koh-i-Noor diamond destroyed the beast with a focussed burst of moonlight, although not before the werewolf had bitten her. After bestowing the Doctor and Rose with knighthoods, Victoria promptly banished them from her kingdom and she established Torchwood to protect the British Empire against further alien attacks.

MONSTER MELEE

Monsters and aliens from all over the universe came together to witness the opening of the Pandorica. Can you find the Doctor, Amy and Rory in this crowd of creatures?

MONSTER MERGE

Aargh, Roman Rory is secretly an Auton!
See if you can identify which monsters
these other friends of the Doctor's
have merged with.

A

B

C

D

CLIFF CODE

The diamond cliffs of Planet One have a message carved into them for the Doctor.
But what does it say? And who is it from?
Crack the code below to find out, by replacing each letter with the one that comes before it in the alphabet.

EPDUPS,
J OFFE
ZPV.
SJWFS
TPOH

◆◆◆◆◆◆ ◆ , ◆◆◆◆ ◆◆◆ ◆ .

THE GALLERY

Add your picture of a beautiful scene or a terrifying monster to this gallery of Vincent van Gogh's incredible paintings!

THE GREY HOLE

The TARDIS has landed on a distant moon...

Come on, Amy – let's explore!

Hang on – what is this place, Doctor?

We're on the Gemstone Moon of Regol Genaralon – look at these flowers! Superb crystalline structure! Completely unique!

It's amazing – but what's that?

Some sort of prefabricated base by the looks of it.

There doesn't appear to be anyone home – it looks deserted!

You're right. This moon rover hasn't been used in weeks – the fuel cells are stone cold.

Hello! Anyo home?!

Whhhuurrrrhhhh!

What was that??

I'm not sure - but it came from inside the dome...

Soon...

A place like this should be busy...

Where is everyone?

According to the data banks, there was a human research team stationed here – but there's been no log entry for two weeks.

So what were they researching?

There it is again! I don't like the sound of it! What's going on here?

We'd better find out – come on!

WHHHUUURRRRHHHH!

The people here have been studying a very rare phenomenon – a Grey Hole!

Grey Hole? I've heard of a Black Hole, Doctor, but...

Well, a Black Hole is a star that's just run out of fuel and collapsed. It's tiny but so heavy that the gravity drags in everything around it – including light.

There are White Holes, too – similar to Black Holes but they sort of operate in reverse, throwing all kinds of stuff out. Some people think they're the other end of Black Holes.

Grey Holes are somewhere in between the two...

...a way of describing a whole range of space-time anomalies that simply should not exist in the universe. At least, not in this one.

And yet there was a team of scientists here investigating one of these Grey Hole things that shouldn't even exist?

Right. Shouldn't exist – but on very rare occasions, they can break through the boundaries between dimensions. They're fabulously rare and incredibly dangerous. Best left well alone, really.

SPOT THE DIFFERENCE

Test your observation skills by finding ten differences between these two pictures of Amy.

WEDDING DAY

On what date are Amy and Rory due to get married? Copy the line in the graph below over the number grid to find out.

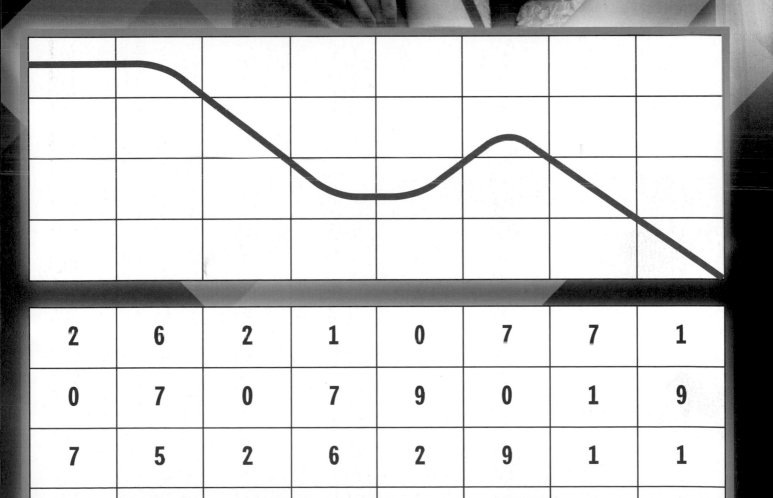

2	6	2	1	0	7	7	1
0	7	0	7	9	0	1	9
7	5	2	6	2	9	1	1
9	0	2	3	4	8	7	0

SECRET OF ARKATRON

Continued from page 63...

Everyone was silent as the Doctor explained. 'Look at the pictures, the videos,' he said. 'They all depict key moments from the time of the Ninth Dynasty of Arkatron.'

'Of course,' the curator said. 'That's what this museum honours.'

'I don't think it honours anything,' the Doctor said. 'The dictators held absolute power and the people were suppressed. Many thousands were executed or simply disappeared.'

'Rule by terror?' Amy said.

The Doctor nodded. 'But that's not the only thing the pictures have in common. There's one figure that appears in them all – depicted in every painting, captured in every photograph, present in every video.'

Amy turned to look at the large painting on the nearby wall – the man being led in chains through a house.

'Yes,' the Doctor said. 'An insignificant little man. So inconsequential you'd barely notice him.

But he's always there. Somewhere.'

'And that's this house,' Amy realised. She turned to the curator. 'You were brought here as a prisoner.'

The little man's eyes had hardened. He pulled a gun from his jacket pocket. 'You're very clever,' he told the Doctor.

'I knew as soon as you said your name was Lester Forge.' The Doctor pointed at the scrolling names. 'Lest You Forget,' he read. 'You used the first words you saw. This isn't a museum – it's a prison. Those are the names of the people you killed. There must be tens of thousands of them. Every book in the library recounts the proceedings of the court that tried you for their deaths.'

'So this place is a monument to them, as well as a prison,' Miss Crisp said.

'Preserving the evidence of what he did,' Professor Landale added.

'And those spooky suits of armour,' Amy said. 'Prison warders?'

The Doctor nodded. 'Disabled when Miss Crisp sabotaged the alarm, except when they detect movement up close. I assume poor Miss Dellman was in charge?' He glanced sadly at the old woman's body.

'The old hag!' the curator snapped. 'As if a frail old crone could keep the great Maxim Klart prisoner!'

'Maxim Klart,' Miss Crisp said. 'Of course – the real power behind the Arkatron dictators. The twisted genius who masterminded the disappearances and the killings.'

Klart laughed. 'Have you any idea how long I had to lie there and watch their names? They thought it would fill me with remorse. It just made me more determined to escape.'

'That's a stasis bed,' the Doctor realised. 'You've been here for years, unable to move. They imprisoned you for ever.'

'I woke when the alarm failed. When Miss Dellman came to check, I took her blaster and killed her. And now I shall kill all of you, unless you give me the access codes for your spaceship.'

'So you can escape and take more lives?' Professor Landale said. 'Never!'

'That's the spirit, Prof,' Amy said.

'Oh, don't be like that,' the Doctor told her. 'Here, I'll unlock my ship for you.' He reached into his jacket pocket.

'Careful,' Klart warned, brandishing the blaster. 'If that's a weapon...'

'As if.' The Doctor took out his sonic screwdriver. 'Here you go.' The screwdriver glowed and whirred. 'That should sort things out.'

'You've never unlocked the TARDIS?' Amy said.

The Doctor grinned. 'Of course not.'

'Then what have you done?' Klart demanded, his face darkening with anger.

'Oh, nothing much. Just reconnected the alarm system, that's all.'

Klart's eyes widened in horror. His finger tightened on the blaster's trigger. But he wasn't quick enough.

Metal hands grabbed him as a robot warder behind Klart lurched into life. All round the room, the suits of armour turned to face their prisoner, advancing menacingly towards him.

'No!' Klart yelled as the blaster was snatched from his hands. 'No – please, you can't let them do this!'

Amy watched in horrified fascination as the robots pushed Klart on to the bed. As soon as he touched it, he seemed to relax. His cries choked off. He fell back, as if asleep.

Except that his eyes were open. As they stared at the scrolling list of people he had sent to die, Klart's eyes were full of terror.

The robot warders stepped back into their alcoves, job done. They were once again as silent

and still as empty suits of armour.

'I think we should leave,' Amy said.

'I couldn't agree more,' the Doctor said.

'Indeed,' Professor Landale said. 'Miss Crisp – we must never tell anyone about this place.'

Miss Crisp agreed. 'No one must find it, or like us they might release the prisoner.'

The Doctor led them all from the room. 'We'll

leave this place as we found it. A monument to the thousands killed by Klart and the dictators of Arkatron.'

A few minutes later the Doctor and Amy stood looking back at the house.

'All those poor people...' Amy said. 'We can never bring them back.'

'No,' the Doctor said sadly. 'But perhaps now they can rest a little bit easier.'

They turned away, heading towards the tiny splash of blue on the horizon that was the TARDIS.

'Come along, Pond,' the Doctor said. 'Our next adventure's waiting.'

The End.

RAGGEDY DOCTOR PUPPET

Amy misses the Time Lord so much while he's away she makes some Raggedy Doctor puppets as a keepsake. Now you can make your very own puppet, too!

You will need:
PVA glue • Plastic bowl • Small cardboard tube • Newspaper • Sticky tape • Toilet paper • Paintbrushes • Paints • Brown wool • Fabric scraps • An adult to help

1 First, you need to make a glue mixture. Add two parts PVA glue to one part water in a bowl and stir together.

2 Next, you need to form the body shape of your puppet. Scrunch up some pieces of newspaper to make two L-shaped legs. Tape them firmly to the inside of the cardboard tube.

3 Make two arms in the same way, and tape these to the sides of the tube.

4 Stuff newspaper inside the cardboard tube and cover the top with sticky tape.

5 Then, scrunch up a small ball of newspaper. Wrap tape around it to hold it together, then tape it to the top of the tube. This will be the head.

6 Layer strips of toilet paper over your figure and use a paintbrush to cover it with glue mixture. Cover the whole body with four layers of paper and glue, then leave it to dry overnight.

7 When your figure has dried hard, it's ready to add the details! Start by painting the head, neck and hands in a flesh colour, and add white paint to the feet as a base for the trainers.

8 Draw in the shoes and face with fine marker pens, then add a mop of woolly hair!

9 Finally, take your scraps of fabric and glue these to the body to make the Doctor's clothes. The messier, the better – this is the Raggedy Doctor, after all!

Make a nose and build up the face with rolled-up pieces of tissue.

You can add pinstripes to his trousers and a pattern on his tie with paint, too.

Use this picture of the Raggedy Doctor to help you design your puppet.

WHO IS HE?

How does the Doctor first describe himself to Amy?
Cross out the answers to the clues below to find out.

Aliens
Places
Words with two letters
Spaceships
Fruit

Weeping Angel	A	Leadworth	Time Lord	of
Starship UK	TARDIS	at	apple	Auton
madman	Dalek	with	Byzantium	Smiler
an	Earth	banana	is	lemon
Cwmtaff	a	Silurian	box	London

ALL A DREAM?

The Dream Lord can make you see things that aren't really true. Take a look at these pairs and circle the real one in each.

ESCAPE!

Race your friends to escape the underground city of the Silurians!

You will need:
- A counter for each player
- A die

How to Play:

The youngest player goes first. Players take it in turns to roll the die and move their playing pieces around the board. Follow the instructions as you go. The first person to reach Earth's surface is the winner.

43 Stung by Silurian venom. Miss a go.	**44**	**45**
42	**41** Take geothermal transport up to the next level. Move on seven spaces.	**40**
29	**30**	**31**
28	**27**	**26**
15	**16** Run from warrior Silurians. Move on two spaces.	**17**
14	**13**	**12**
START	**2**	**3**

FINISH

46	47	48	**49** Roll a one to reach the surface!
39	38	37	36
32	33	34	35
25 iscover hibernating ilurians. Miss a go.	24	23	22
18	19	20	21
11	10	**9** Stop to look at the archives. Miss a go.	8
4	5	6	7

ANSWERS

Page 22 - The Legend Revealed

		A	M	Y		P	O	N	D				
	E	T	E	R	N	A	L						
		B	Y	Z	A	N	T	I	U	M			
			G	U	I	D	O						
D	R	E	A	M	L	O	R	D					
			S	T	A	R	S	H	I	P	U	K	
			D	R	I	L	L						
	C	H	U	R	C	H	I	L	L				
		A	T	R	A	X	I						

Page 23 - Who's There?

A. Silurian
B. Dalek
C. Weeping Angel
D. Winder

Page 30 - Giant Word Search

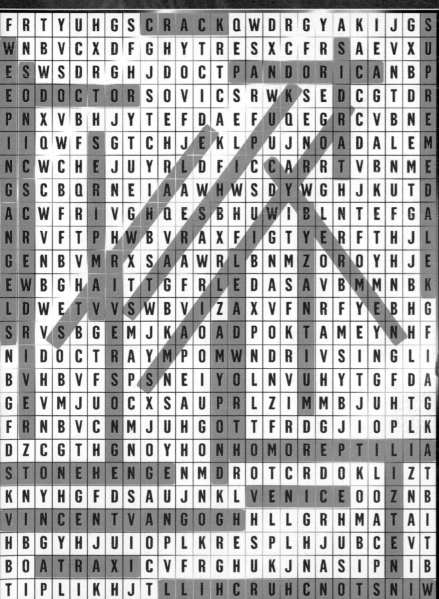

Page 70 – Monster Merge

A. Dalek   B. Silurian
C. Vampire   D. Weeping Angel

Page 72 – Cliff Code

The message reads:
Doctor, I need you. River Song.

Page 80 – Spot the Difference

Page 81 – Wedding Day

The date is 26/06/2010.

2	6	2	1	0	7	7	1
0	7	0	7	9	0	1	9
7	5	2	6	2	9	1	1
9	0	2	3	4	8	7	0

Page 87 – All a Dream?

Page 86 – Who is He?

A madman with a box.

Weeping Angel	A	Leadworth	Time Lord	X
Starship UK	TARDIS	X	apple	Adam
madman	Dalek	with	Byzantium	Spitfire
X	Earth	banana	X	lemon
Cwmtaff	a	Silurian	box	London